Congratula

Engagement

Carole Dane
& Family.

July 2001

MOOD FOOD

MOOD FOOD

hamlyn

First published in 2000 by Hamlyn
an imprint of Octopus Publishing Group Limited
2–4 Heron Quays, London E14 4JP

British Library Cataloguing-in-Publication Data
A catalogue record for this book is available from
the British Library

ISBN 0 600 59855 1

Printed in China

Creative Director	Keith Martin
Executive Art Editor	Leigh Jones
Senior Designer	David Godfrey
Production Controller	Lisa Moore
Editor	Sarah Ford
Assistant Editor	Sharon Ashman
Picture Researcher	Rosie Garai
Special Photography	Paul White
Model	Kirsten Symonds
Stylist	Akoiko

Acknowledgements

Decadent chapter shot on location at
Carolyn Corben's flat, for enquiries about
bed linen used in this chapter phone
The New Renaissance, 0207 240 8302.
Romantic chapter shot on location at
The Savoy Hotel, The Strand, London
WC2R OEU, to make a reservation at
the hotel or River Restaurant or for
any other enquiries phone 0207 836 4343.
Wild chapter shot on location at Shari
and Bill Maryon's house, Bristol.

Picture Acknowledgements

Arena Images/ Hanyachlala 107
Image Bank/ Antonio Rosario 67
The Interior Archive/ Simon Brown 130
Octopus Publishing Group Ltd. /Jean Cazals 13,
28,133 /Gus Filgate 124 /Colin Gott 91,122 /Sandra
Lane 2 right, 4-5, 7, 12, 18-19, 19, 40, 41, 42, 45,
49, 52, 58, 62, 68, 79, 81, 82 Top, 90, 95, 102, 105,
121, 127, 131, 135 /Gary Latham 34-35, 46 /David
Loftus 3, 11, 17, 24, 47, 64, 66, 86, 92, 93, 97, 101,
104, 106, 109, 112, 123 /James Merrell 27, 100
/Neil Mersh 32, 33, 57, 59, 114, 140, 141 /Hilary
Moore 51, 110 /Peter Myers 103 /Sean Myers 31,
37, 56, 71, 99, 119 /Peter Pugh-Cook 36 /William
Reavell 1, 6, 16, 23, 50, 53, 73, 84, 87, 94, 96, 111,
113, 115, 118, 125 /Salvatore 60, 75, 88-89, 134,
138 /Simon Smith 132 /Ian Wallace 21, 48, 63, 65,
68-69, 70, 72, 76, 78, 80, 82-83 /Philip Webb Front
Cover, 15, 38, 44, 55, 74, 77, 85, 129, 137, 139
Tony Stone Images/ Bob Krist 108

Notes

- Standard level spoon measurements are used in all recipes.
  1 tablespoon = one 15 ml spoon
  1 teaspoon = one 5 ml spoon
- Imperial and metric measurements have been given in all recipes. Use one set of measurements only and not a mixture of both.
- Eggs should be medium unless otherwise stated.
- Milk should be full fat unless otherwise stated.
- Pepper should be freshly ground unless otherwise stated.
- Fresh herbs should be used unless otherwise stated. If unavailable use dried herbs as an alternative but halve the given quantities.
- Ovens should be preheated to the specified temperature – if using a fan assisted oven, follow the manufacturer's instructions for adjusting the time and temperature.

Contents

Introduction

A mood is simply a state of mind, our moods affect everything we do and the way we do it, and particularly what we feel like doing. You might, for example, feel in a particularly wild state of mind, tempted by the idea of taking on new challenges and attempting something that you've never had the nerve to try before. Or you might be totally at ease with the world and feel like putting your feet up, spending a quiet time and allowing nothing to intrude on your relaxed mood. Or you may feel eager for a decadent, self-indulgent bout of pampering in the way that you are sure you deserve. Or perhaps you are in an active, energetic, get-up-and-go frame of mind, with a wish list for an hour in the gym, a brisk walk in the park and getting to grips with all those pressing jobs that you've been meaning to finish for weeks. Or you may even be in the mood for love, with dreams of romance and quiet evenings alone together.

Go with the flow

Our moods are influenced by a whole host of factors. These include the weather, the time of year and the foods we've been eating, but, more importantly, the people around us. An argument for example, can change your mood, or a smile from someone in the street. Even the post you receive can change the way you are feeling. However you feel, it's always important to allow yourself to be led by your mood. Let yourself be guided by the way you feel because, if you try to do something at odds with your mood, you're unlikely to do it well. A little of what you fancy does you good, so wear what you feel like, do what you want, and cook whatever takes your fancy.

Changing moods

Moods can change unexpectedly. Just because yesterday you were in an active frame of mind, doesn't mean that you'll feel the same today. Perhaps now a new day has dawned, you favour a relaxed mood, with nothing on the agenda other than sitting and reflecting.

Your mood is perhaps the most influential thing in your life. It can affect everything you do and the way in which you do it. This also applies to the food you want to eat and the way you want to cook. We've taken five moods – decadent, active, relaxed, wild and romantic – and suggested things you will feel like cooking when you are in those moods.

A decadent mood

Everyone needs to be pampered from time to time, and food is one of the most effective ways of doing this. So if you're feeling deliciously decadent, go on and spoil yourself. You will find dishes in this chapter that are laced in luxury and extravagance to delight your taste buds and give you a lift.

Try Rich Polenta Salad, for example, which succeeds in putting the wickedness back into salad, or for a real treat, make Peppered Tuna Steaks with Fennel, Red Onions and Sugar Snaps, and delight in a colourful medley of flavours. Chicken with Cream Cheese, Garlic and Herbs elevates this ubiquitous meat to something rich, luxurious and utterly delicious. Chocoholics are bound to agree that Hot Chocolate Crêpes were invented in heaven. And, as if that wasn't enough, there is also a wildly extravagant Champagne cocktail with vodka, peach schnapps and peach juice, which is the ultimate in self-indulgence.

An active mood

Full of beans and raring to go? Now's the time to dash into the kitchen and create something wonderful. When you're feeling active, you'll want to stun your senses with crunchy textures, dazzling colours and startling flavours to maintain that energy high. None of the recipes in this section take long to prepare and before you know it, you'll find yourself cooking up a sensational spread of delectable dishes.

There's nothing quite like griddling to get you on your feet, or like lemon to activate all the senses, so try Griddled Tiger Prawns with Mint and Lemon and you'll be ready for anything. Or perhaps you'd rather surprise your taste buds with Spicy Beef Koftas in Pizzaiola Sauce, in which chilli and garlic share pride of place. When you use up lots of energy, then you need long refreshing drinks. Limeade and Grapefruit Mint Cooler taste great and put you back on top of the world.

A relaxed mood

Cooking is fun but slaving over a hot stove is quite definitely not. For those days when you are feeling laid back and relaxed, you want to cook something that is easy and, preferably, quite speedy. Quick doesn't have to be boring – far from it – and the clever cook will be able to concoct something utterly delicious, high on flavour but low on labour, which you will then be able to savour in a hammock in the garden, or in front of your favourite film.

Try Grilled Radicchio and Fontina Bruschetta with Anchovy Relish, for example, which will take you just fifteen minutes and yet get your taste buds buzzing with pleasure. Or rustle up a quick pasta dish of Fettucine with Smoked Salmon and Asparagus Sauce, which takes less than half an hour to prepare. Risotto is always tasty, but many people dismiss it as being too complicated and time-consuming to prepare. Just allow yourself to be taken over by the repetitive stirring process, and you'll be surprised at how much more relaxed you feel when you dig into the delicious end product than when you started. And to take the final curtain, Bananas in Coconut Milk take just minutes to prepare for a truly scrumptious dessert. So unwind, relax, and enjoy yourself!

A wild mood

There will be days when you're in the mood for being wild and want an adventure, when you feel like a challenge and you've got more than the usual time and energy to spare. Trying out an entirely new, untested recipe can present you with a welcome challenge.

Try Steamboat Soup from Cambodia, for example, and serve an out-of-the-ordinary, cook-at-the-table hotpot of poached seafood in an aromatic stock of startlingly tart ingredients, garnished with coriander and sweet basil leaves and slices of chilli. Or take a trip to Tunisia and serve deep-fried filo turnovers, called briks, or try your hand at Lamb Tagine with Okra and Almonds, flavoured with a subtle mixture of garlic, ginger, spices and honey. Thailand has a lot of ideas for the wild cook, and Crisp Fried Fish with Chilli and Basil is sure to please the most discerning eater. Finally, go to India for the close of play, with delicious ice creams flavoured with pistachio and saffron and decorated with edible gold or silver leaf.

A romantic mood

Certain foods are well known for their passionate persuasions, such as prawns and oysters, chillies, asparagus and chocolate and when you are feeling romantic, nothing else will do. The recipes in this chapter are sensuous and tantalizing for those evenings for two, whether it is a candle-lit supper or a cosy night on the sofa. All are quick to prepare to allow you more time with your loved one, and less in the kitchen alone.

Conjure up a Mexican Soup with Avocado Salsa, for example, a fiery dish to arouse the passions, which reflects the rich colours and contrasting moods of Latin America, cooled by the subtle smoothness of an avocado salsa. Oysters are well known for their aphrodisiac qualities, so we suggest you try Devilled Oysters and see if they live up to their reputation. If you're having a quiet evening in, we suggest you cuddle up on the sofa together and share a plate of scrumptious Crispy Wrapped Prawns. Lobster has always had sexy connotations, so try Griddled Lobster Tails with Oregano Butter for a special occasion – with luck, you'll agree it was worth the expense. And for afters, we suggest Passion Cake, which is so-called for a very good reason. Wash it down with Blue Champagne, the ultimate in romantic drinks.

Decadent

If your mood is one of utter decadence, this chapter is for you. It's sure to provide you with all the ideas that you need to indulge yourself shamelessly. You will find dishes here to pamper your taste buds, and a choice of luxurious, wicked foods to linger over and luxuriate in, with the creamiest sauces, the richest cheeses and – needless to say – the smoothest, most sensuous chocolate flavours. And as if that wasn't enough, there are also some extravagant cocktail recipes with which to give yourself the occasional lift. So give yourself up to the delights of these tempting recipes and spoil yourself.

Rich polenta salad

These bars of polenta and goats' cheese – rich and creamy, thick and buttery – are just the thing to add a touch of luxury and excitement to your salads.

600 ml (1 pint) water
150 g (5 oz) quick-cooking polenta flour
25 g (1 oz) butter
250 g (8 oz) goats' cheese, rinded
1 small radicchio head, separated into leaves
125 g (4 oz) rocket
3 tablespoons extra virgin olive oil
1 tablespoon balsamic vinegar
salt and pepper

1 Heat the water to a gentle simmer, pour in the polenta flour and beat well for 1–2 minutes until it is a smooth paste. Turn the heat down and continue to cook the polenta until it thickens, stirring constantly so that it does not catch on the bottom of the pan or form a skin on the top; it needs to cook in this way for 6–8 minutes.

2 When the polenta is thick and cooked, add the butter and season with salt and pepper; mix well. Pour it on to a chopping board and spread to 1.5 cm (¾ inch) thick and allow to set for 5 minutes.

3 Thinly slice or crumble the goats' cheese and spread it on the polenta, then cut the polenta into bars or wedges. Place the polenta under a preheated hot grill and cook until the cheese has melted and started to bubble.

4 Put the radicchio leaves and the rocket into a bowl. Add the oil and vinegar and season with salt and pepper, then toss the leaves until coated. Arrange the salad leaves on individual plates and place the polenta bars on top.

Baked reblochon

A crisp puff-pastry case, bursting with rich, bubbling cheese, will make one of life's magical moments.

12

250 g (8 oz) puff pastry, defrosted if frozen
1 small Reblochon cheese
1 egg yolk mixed with 1 tablespoon water
sweet chutney, to serve

Oven temperature: 220°C (425°F), Gas Mark 7

1 Divide the pastry in half and roll each half out on a lightly floured surface to form a thin square.

2 Take the cheese and, using a very sharp knife, cut away the rind. Sit the Reblochon in the middle of one pastry square, brush around the cheese with a little egg yolk mixture and then top with the second pastry square. Press all around the edges to seal well and then trim the pastry to give a 2.5 cm (1 inch) border.

3 Transfer the pastry to a baking sheet and leave to chill for 30 minutes. Brush the top and sides with more of the egg yolk mixture and score the top with a sharp knife to form a criss-cross pattern. Cut 2 small slits in the top of the pastry to allow the steam to escape.

4 Bake in a preheated oven, 220°C (425°F), Gas Mark 7, for 20 minutes until the pastry is puffed up and golden. Allow to stand for about 10 minutes, then cut into wedges and serve with chutney.

Spicy courgette fritters

Serve these spicy courgette fritters as a special treat, topped with smoked salmon and soured cream.

500 g (1 lb) courgettes, grated

1 egg, beaten

2 tablespoons plain flour

1 chilli, deseeded and chopped

1 garlic clove, crushed

75 g (3 oz) Cheddar cheese, grated

salt and pepper

dill sprigs, to garnish

To serve:

175 g (6 oz) smoked salmon

150 ml (¼ pint) soured cream

1 Heat a griddle pan or nonstick frying pan. Squeeze the excess moisture out of the grated courgettes – the best way to do this is to place all the courgettes into a clean tea towel and squeeze well.

2 Mix together the egg and flour until smooth. Add the courgettes, chilli, garlic and cheese, mix well and season to taste with salt and pepper.

3 Place spoonfuls of the mixture on to the hot pan, flatten with a palette knife and cook the fritters for 4–5 minutes, then turn and cook for a further 4–5 minutes. Do not disturb them while they are cooking as a crust needs to form on the cooking side, otherwise they will be difficult to turn.

4 Keep the cooked fritters warm and repeat until all the mixture has been used. Serve the fritters between layers of smoked salmon and soured cream, and garnish with sprigs of dill.

Variation: Spicy Potato Fritters

Replace the courgettes with 500 g (1 lb) peeled and grated potatoes. Squeeze the moisture out of the potatoes and make the fritters following the main recipe.

Sichuan scallops

16

This recipe hails from the region of Sichuan in western China. Hot and fiery, it is intended for the boldest palates.

2 tablespoons oil

750 g (1½ lb) scallops

2 garlic cloves, crushed

1 dried red chilli, finely chopped

½ teaspoon Chinese five spice powder

2.5 cm (1 inch) piece of fresh root ginger, peeled and finely shredded

2 tablespoons Chinese rice wine or dry sherry

2 tablespoons dark soy sauce

3 tablespoons water

6 spring onions, diagonally sliced

1 small onion, sliced

1 teaspoon caster sugar

2 spring onions, shredded, to garnish

1   Heat the oil in a wok or heavy-based frying pan until smoking hot. Add the scallops and sear on both sides, then remove and reserve.

2   Add the garlic, chilli, five spice powder and ginger and stir-fry for 1 minute. Add the wine or sherry, soy sauce, water, spring onions, onion and caster sugar and stir-fry for 1 minute more, then return the scallops to the wok and stir-fry them in the sauce for no longer than 2 minutes or they will become tough.

3   Arrange the scallops with their sauce on a warmed serving dish and garnish with the spring onions.

Peppered tuna steaks with fennel, red onions and sugar snaps

1 First prepare the vegetables. Remove the feathery fronds from the fennel bulbs, chop finely and reserve. Trim the root ends of the fennel and discard. Cut the fennel in half lengthways, then cut into 5 mm (¼ inch) thick slices. Cut the onions into rings. Top and tail the sugar snaps or mangetout and cut in half lengthways on the diagonal. Peel the potatoes.

2 Heat the oil and butter in a large frying pan, fry the fennel slices gently for 5 minutes, then add the onions. Cook over a moderate heat until the fennel and onions are tender, then increase the heat to colour slightly. Remove from the heat and keep warm. Boil the potatoes until tender.

3 Meanwhile, coarsely crush the peppercorns with a pestle or the end of a rolling pin. Mix with the salt. Brush the tuna steaks with the olive oil and press in the pepper mixture to coat. Heat a large frying pan over a moderate heat. Set the steaks in the dry pan and fry for 2 minutes on one side, then turn and fry for 1 minute on the second side.

4 Add the sugar snaps or mangetout to the fennel and onion mixture with the fennel fronds and toss over a high heat until hot. Drain the potatoes, cut each one into 4–5 slices and keep warm. Transfer the tuna to a warmed dish and keep warm.

5 Turn the heat up under the frying pan. Add any remaining cracked pepper, pour on the brandy and a little of the stock and stir to scrape up the sediment and any fish juices. Let the mixture bubble fiercely for a few seconds, then add the rest of the stock and the lemon juice and boil rapidly until syrupy.

6 Remove the frying pan from the heat and gradually add the butter pieces, stirring to combine them with the sauce and thicken it. Add the cream, still stirring to mix well. Bring to the boil and boil for a few seconds, then add the chopped parsley and reduce the heat. Keep warm while serving the fish.

7 Divide the vegetables between 4 warmed plates, arranging them in a mound in the centre. Set a tuna steak on this and pour a little of the peppered sauce on top of each steak and around the edge of the vegetables. Garnish with parsley sprigs and serve immediately.

Tuna is a firm, meaty fish, well deserving of this exciting treatment with an interesting mêlée of garden vegetables.

19

4 tablespoons black peppercorns
1 teaspoon salt
4 x 150 g (5 oz) tuna steaks
1 tablespoon olive oil
50 ml (2 fl oz) brandy
150 ml (¼ pint) concentrated fish or
   chicken stock
3 tablespoons lemon juice
50 g (2 oz) unsalted butter, cut into small dice
150 ml (¼ pint) double cream
2 tablespoons finely chopped parsley
4 flat leaf parsley sprigs, to garnish

Vegetables:
2 fennel bulbs
2 red onions
125 g (4 oz) sugar snap peas or mangetout
4 potatoes
2 tablespoons olive oil
25 g (1 oz) unsalted butter

Fish in wine sauce

Make this delicately flavoured dish with lemon sole or plaice, or try sea bass fillets if you want a more robust texture.

375 g (12 oz) white fish fillets, skinned

1 egg white

2 garlic cloves, finely chopped

1 tablespoon cornflour

300 ml (½ pint) groundnut oil

salt and pepper

1 tablespoon chopped coriander leaves, to garnish

a few drops of chilli oil, to serve

Wine sauce:

250 ml (8 fl oz) hot chicken stock

6 tablespoons Chinese rice wine or dry sherry

1 tablespoon cornflour

½ teaspoon sugar

2 tablespoons chopped coriander leaves

1   Cut the fish into bite-sized pieces. Put the egg white and garlic into a bowl with salt and pepper to taste and whisk with a fork until frothy. Sift in the cornflour and whisk to mix, then add the fish and stir until coated.

2   Heat the oil in a wok until very hot but not smoking. Deep-fry the fish in batches for about 2 minutes each until crisp and lightly golden. Lift out with a slotted spoon and drain on kitchen paper. Very carefully pour off all the hot oil from the wok and wipe the wok clean with kitchen paper.

3   Next make the sauce. Pour the stock and rice wine or sherry into the wok and bring to the boil over a high heat. Blend the cornflour to a paste with a little cold water, then pour it into the wok and stir to mix. Simmer, stirring, for 2 minutes until thickened.

4   Add the sugar and stir to dissolve, then stir in the chopped coriander. Return the fish to the wok. Stir the fish very gently to coat it in the sauce and heat through for 1–2 minutes, then taste for seasoning and add more sugar, if liked. Serve very hot with a few drops of chilli oil and garnished with coriander leaves.

Chicken with cream cheese, garlic and herbs

Chicken breasts are tender and special any time, but this herb, garlic and cream cheese stuffing nestling between the skin and flesh, makes them ultra-special.

4 chicken breasts

125 g (4 oz) cream cheese or low-fat soft cheese

3 tablespoons finely chopped mixed herbs (such as tarragon, dill, parsley, chervil)

1–2 garlic cloves, crushed

15 g (½ oz) butter

salt and pepper

green salad, to serve

To garnish:

lemon wedges

rosemary sprigs

Oven temperature: 220°C (425°F), Gas Mark 7

1 Insert your fingers between the skin and the flesh of each chicken breast to make a pocket.

2 Put the cheese in a bowl with the herbs, garlic and salt and pepper to taste. Beat well to mix. Push the cheese mixture into the pockets in the chicken breasts, dividing it equally between them. Smooth the skin over the cheese to make it as compact as possible.

3 Melt the butter in a small saucepan, then use to brush a baking dish. Arrange the chicken breasts in a single layer in the dish, then brush with the remaining butter and season to taste with salt and pepper.

4 Cook in a preheated oven, 220°C (425°F), Gas Mark 7, for 20 minutes or until the chicken is cooked through and tender when pierced with a skewer or fork.

5 Serve the chicken hot, cut diagonally into slices if liked, garnished with lemon and rosemary sprigs. A green salad would make a good accompaniment.

Stuffed baked lamb

This is a magnificent Moroccan dish – just the thing for those occasions when you want to entertain a crowd in style.

2 kg (4 lb) boned leg of lamb
1 onion, cut into thick wedges
3 tablespoons olive oil
8 tablespoons lemon juice
green beans, to serve

Stuffing:

50 g (2 oz) couscous
150 ml (¼ pint) boiling water
2 teaspoons coriander seeds
2 teaspoons cumin seeds
1 teaspoon ground cinnamon
3 tablespoons olive oil
50 g (2 oz) pine nuts
50 g (2 oz) flaked almonds
1 large onion, finely chopped
2 garlic cloves, crushed
1 teaspoon dried mint
4 tablespoons chopped coriander leaves
50 g (2 oz) raisins
salt and pepper

Oven temperature: 240°C (475°F), Gas Mark 9

1 First make the stuffing. Put the couscous into a bowl, pour over the boiling water, stir then leave until the water has been absorbed.

2 Heat a small heavy-based pan, add the coriander and cumin seeds and heat until fragrant. Grind to a powder then mix with the cinnamon.

3 Heat 1 tablespoon of the oil in a frying pan, add the pine nuts and almonds and fry until browned. Transfer to kitchen paper to drain. Add the remaining oil to the pan. When it is hot, add the onion and fry until soft. Stir in the garlic and spice mixture and fry for 2 minutes, then add the couscous, nuts, mint, coriander, raisins and salt and pepper to taste.

4 Open out the lamb, skin side down, on a work surface. Season inside with pepper then spread over the stuffing. If possible, tuck the flaps of the piece of lamb over the stuffing. Roll up the lamb into a neat sausage shape then tie securely with string.

5 Put the onion wedges into a roasting tin that the lamb will just fit. Put the lamb on the onion and pour over the oil and lemon juice. Place in a preheated oven, 240°C (475°F), Gas Mark 9, and bake for 15 minutes. Lower the oven temperature to 220°C (425°F), Gas Mark 7, and bake for a further 25 minutes so the lamb is still pink in the centre. Remove the lamb from the oven, cover and leave to stand in a warm place for about 15 minutes before carving. Serve with green beans.

Venison cutlets with red juniper pears

Pears in red wine, usually a dessert, are also excellent served with rich venison cutlets to make a memorable meal.

4 firm dessert pears
2 tablespoons lemon juice
300 ml (½ pint) red wine
6 juniper berries, crushed
pared rind of 1 lemon, cut into julienne strips
1 cinnamon stick
3 tablespoons redcurrant jelly
8 venison cutlets
oil or melted butter
watercress sprigs, to serve

1   Peel the pears, then halve them lengthways and remove each core with a melon baller. Brush the flesh with the lemon juice to prevent the pears from discolouring.

2   Combine the wine, juniper berries, lemon rind and cinnamon stick in a saucepan. Bring to the boil, add the pears, cover and simmer gently for 10 minutes or until tender.

3   Transfer the pears to a bowl with a slotted spoon and set aside. Stir the redcurrant jelly into the liquid remaining in the pan and boil until reduced by half. Pour over the pears and leave to cool.

4   Brush the venison with a little oil or butter. Cook under a hot grill or on a barbecue for 2–3 minutes on each side. To serve, place 2 cutlets on each plate and add a portion of pears. Serve with sprigs of watercress.

Zuccotto

This is a luxury dessert par excellence. The traditional decoration for zuccotto is one of alternate stripes of icing sugar and cocoa powder sifted over the dessert.

3 large eggs

75 g (3 oz) caster sugar

50 g (2 oz) flour

1 tablespoon cocoa powder, plus extra
   for dusting

1 tablespoon oil

Filling:

4 tablespoons brandy

350 ml (12 fl oz) double cream

40 g (1½ oz) icing sugar, sifted

50 g (2 oz) plain chocolate, chopped

25 g (1 oz) almonds, chopped and toasted

175 g (6 oz) cherries, pitted

2 tablespoons Kirsch

Oven temperature: 180°C (350°F), Gas Mark 4

1 Place the eggs and caster sugar in a heatproof bowl and whisk over a saucepan of hot water until thick. Sift the flour and cocoa powder into the bowl and fold into the egg mixture, then fold in the oil.

2 Spoon into a greased 20 cm (8 inch) cake tin and bake in a preheated oven, 180°C (350°F), Gas Mark 4, for 35–40 minutes. Turn on to a wire rack to cool.

3 When cool, cut the sponge in half horizontally and line a 1.8 litre (3 pint) bowl with one layer. Sprinkle with brandy. Whip the cream to soft peaks. Fold in 25 g (1 oz) of the icing sugar, the chocolate, almonds, cherries and Kirsch. Spoon into the bowl and top with the remaining sponge. Cover with a plate and chill.

4 Turn out on to a serving plate, then sprinkle with the remaining icing sugar and cocoa powder to make a pattern.

Hot chocolate crêpes

As any chocoholic would agree, there is nothing more luxurious than these pancakes, sinking in a hot chocolate sauce.

Crêpes:

100 g (3½ oz) **plain flour**

15 g (½ oz) **cocoa powder**

2 tablespoons **caster sugar**

1 **egg**

300 ml (½ pint) **milk**

oil, for frying

Filling:

1 piece **stem ginger (weighing about 15 g/½ oz)**

2 tablespoons **caster sugar**

250 g (8 oz) **ricotta cheese**

50 g (2 oz) **raisins**

150 g (5 oz) **white chocolate, finely chopped**

3 tablespoons **double cream**

Chocolate sauce:

125 g (4 oz) **caster sugar**

125 ml (4 fl oz) **cold water**

175 g (6 oz) **plain chocolate, broken into pieces**

25 g (1 oz) **unsalted butter**

2 tablespoons **brandy (optional)**

Oven temperature: 200°C (400°F), Gas Mark 6

1 First make the crêpes. Sift the flour and cocoa powder into a mixing bowl. Stir in the sugar. Add the egg and a little milk, and whisk to make a stiff batter. Beat in the remaining milk.

2 Heat a little oil in a medium frying pan, then pour off the excess. When the pan is very hot, pour in a little batter and tilt the pan so the batter coats the base. Cook over a moderate heat until browned on the underside.

3 Flip over the crêpe with a palette knife and cook the other side. Slide the crêpe out of the pan and keep warm while you make 7 more crêpes.

4 To make the filling, finely chop the ginger and mix in a bowl with the sugar, ricotta, raisins, chocolate and cream. Place a spoonful of the filling in the centre of each crêpe. Fold into quarters, enclosing the filling.

5 Arrange the crêpes in a shallow ovenproof dish then bake in a preheated oven, 200°C (400°F), Gas Mark 6, for 10 minutes until heated through.

6 Meanwhile, make the chocolate sauce. Heat the sugar and water in a small heavy-based saucepan until the sugar has dissolved. Bring to the boil and boil for 1 minute. Remove from the heat and stir in the chocolate and butter. Stir until dissolved, then add the brandy, if using. Serve with the crêpes.

Bellini-tini

32

This slightly effervescent mixture of vodka, peach schnapps, peach juice and Champagne is the ultimate in self-indulgence.

2 measures vodka
½ measure peach schnapps
1 teaspoon peach juice
Champagne, to top up
peach slices, to decorate

1 Pour the vodka, peach schnapps and peach juice into a cocktail shaker. Shake thoroughly. Pour into a cocktail glass and top up with Champagne. Decorate with the peach slices.

Sapphire martini

33

The piercing blue of Curaçao speaks volumes about luxury. Add a cocktail cherry and you couldn't ask for more.

ice cubes

2 measures gin

½ measure blue Curaçao

1 red or blue cocktail cherry (optional)

1   Put the ice cubes into a cocktail shaker. Pour in the gin and blue Curaçao. Shake well to mix. Strain into a cocktail glass and carefully drop in a cocktail cherry, if using.

active

You're bursting with energy and raring to go, so now's the time to whip up a storm in the kitchen. None of these dishes will take long to prepare and they will get you singing and dancing your way around the kitchen at the drop of a whisk. You won't sit still for a minute because there's no rest for the wicked and you'll be quite literally chopping, slicing, dicing, stirring, blending, griddling, firing up your wok and lighting those coals. Bright colours, contrasting textures and dazzling flavours will all shock your taste buds into action and keep you feeling full of beans, fighting fit and overflowing with energy.

Yellow pepper and tomato pizza

The contrasting textures and colours of the brightest yellow peppers and red cherry tomatoes are sure to put a spring into your step.

2 large ripe tomatoes, sliced

125 g (4 oz) red cherry tomatoes, halved

125 g (4 oz) yellow peppers, deseeded and sliced

4 sun-dried tomatoes in oil, drained and sliced (optional)

2 teaspoons grated lemon rind

12 black olives, pitted

olive oil, for oiling and drizzling

salt and pepper

basil leaves, to garnish

Pizza dough:

250 g (8 oz) strong plain flour, plus extra for kneading

½ teaspoon salt

½ teaspoon fast-action dried yeast

125 ml (4 fl oz) warm water

1 tablespoon olive oil

Oven temperature: 230°C (450°F), Gas Mark 8

1 To make the dough, sift the flour and salt into a large bowl and stir in the yeast. Make a well in the centre and gradually stir in the water and oil to form a soft dough. Turn out on to a lightly floured surface and knead for 8–10 minutes until smooth and elastic. Place in an oiled bowl. Turn the dough once to coat the surface with oil, then cover with oiled clingfilm. Leave to rise in a warm place for 45 minutes, or until doubled in size.

2 Knead the dough lightly and divide into 2 equal pieces. Roll out each piece of dough to a 23 cm (9 inch) round and transfer to 2 oiled pizza plates or a large oiled baking sheet.

3 Arrange the tomatoes, yellow pepper, sun-dried tomatoes, if using, lemon rind and olives over the dough. Season well with salt and pepper and drizzle with a little olive oil.

4 Bake at the top of a preheated oven, 230°C (450°F), Gas Mark 8, for 20 minutes or until the bases are crisp and the top golden. Garnish with the basil leaves and serve hot or cold.

active

There's nothing that will keep your spirits up quite like a dish full of freshness and vitality. Griddling is fun, so get to it ...

Griddled aubergines

4 aubergines, sliced into rounds, or baby
   aubergines, sliced lengthways
1 large bunch of basil
75 g (3 oz) pine nuts, toasted
1 garlic clove
75 g (3 oz) Parmesan cheese, grated
grated rind of 2 lemons
4 tablespoons lemon juice
3 tablespoons olive oil
salt and pepper

38

1   Heat a griddle pan or nonstick frying pan until hot.
    Place the aubergine slices on the pan and cook for
    3 minutes on each side, then remove and arrange
    on a serving dish. Repeat until all the aubergines
    are cooked.

2   To make the lemon pesto, place the basil, pine nuts,
    garlic, Parmesan, lemon rind and juice and olive oil
    in a food processor or blender, season with salt and
    pepper and process until smooth.

3   Drizzle the lemon pesto over the aubergines and
    serve with crusty bread.

Variation: Griddled Courgettes with Lemon Pesto

Use courgettes instead of aubergines, cut them lengthways into thick ribbons, and cook as in the main recipe.
Serve drizzled with lemon pesto.

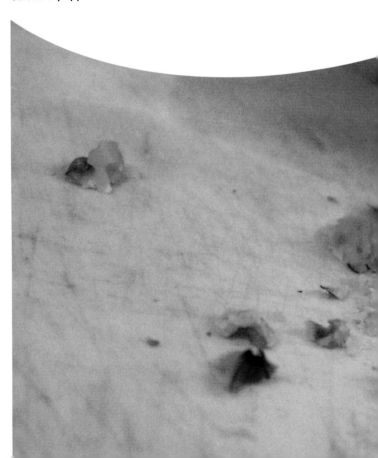

with lemon pesto

active

Vegetable beignets

750 g (1½ lb) assorted vegetables, such as peppers, courgettes,
  aubergines, baby sweetcorn, onions, French beans, cauliflower,
  mushrooms
sunflower oil, for frying
herb sprigs or salad leaves, to garnish
garlic mayonnaise or sweet and sour sauce, to serve

Serve this varied medley of
fresh vegetables in crisp, puffy
Japanese tempura batter
with garlic mayonnaise or
with sweet and sour sauce.
Your taste buds will be
working overtime.

Tempura batter:

1 large egg
200 ml (7 fl oz) lager, very well chilled
125 g (4 oz) plain flour
½ teaspoon baking powder
salt and pepper

Oven temperature: 190°C (375°F), Gas Mark 5

1 Cut the peppers lengthways into 5 mm (¼ inch) thick strips. Cut the courgettes into flat batons about 3 mm (⅛ inch) thick and the aubergines into slices on the diagonal about 3 mm (⅛ inch) thick. Cut the baby sweetcorn in half lengthways, the onions into thin rings and the French beans into 4 cm (1½ inch) lengths. Cut the cauliflower into florets and parboil them for 2 minutes. Drain and refresh. Leave the mushrooms whole if small, or cut in half if large.

2 About 20 minutes before cooking, prepare the batter. With a small wire whisk, beat the egg in a large bowl. Still beating, add the lager in a thin stream. Sift the flour, baking powder and a pinch of salt into another bowl, stir in pepper to taste and tip on top of the egg and lager. Stir with the whisk, barely enough to mix; don't overbeat. Cover and leave to stand for about 10 minutes.

3 Heat the oil to 190°C (375°F), or until a cube of bread browns in 30 seconds. Dip the vegetables in the batter, one type at a time. Fry no more than 6 pieces at once or the temperature of the oil will drop and make the batter greasy. Courgettes, onions, cauliflower, baby sweetcorn and mushrooms take 3–5 minutes; peppers, aubergines and beans about 3 minutes. The batter should be puffy, crisp and golden, the vegetables just tender.

4 Transfer the vegetables to an ovenproof dish or tray lined with kitchen paper and keep warm in a preheated oven, 190°C (375°F), Gas Mark 5, until they are all cooked. They will stay crisp for about 30 minutes.

5 Arrange the beignets on a large platter around a bowl of sauce, or pile about 9 beignets in the centre of each individual plate and put a few spoonfuls of sauce on the side. Garnish with herbs or salad leaves and serve immediately.

Griddled tiger prawns with mint and lemon

There's nothing quite like griddling to get you dancing in the kitchen, or like lemon to activate the senses!

750 g (1½ lb) raw tiger prawns peeled, heads removed and deveined

1 large bunch of mint, chopped

2 garlic cloves, crushed

8 tablespoons lemon juice

sea salt and pepper

mint leaves, to garnish

1   Place the prawns in a glass mixing bowl. Add the mint, garlic and lemon juice to the prawns, season with salt and pepper and allow to marinate for 30 minutes or overnight.

2   Heat a griddle pan or nonstick frying pan until hot. Place the prawns and marinade on the pan and cook for 2–3 minutes on each side. Serve garnished with mint leaves.

Spicy baked fish

A firm, meaty fish stuffed with a tangy mixture of herbs and breadcrumbs and topped with garlic and chilli – an assault on the senses, but a welcome one.

1.5–2 kg (3–4 lb) sea bass or bream, cleaned, scaled and filleted

juice of 2 limes

6 tablespoons olive oil

deep-fried onion rings, to garnish

Stuffing:

125 g (4 oz) soft breadcrumbs

50 g (2 oz) butter, melted

1 tablespoon finely chopped chives

1 teaspoon finely chopped coriander

1 small green pepper, cored, deseeded and finely chopped

½ onion, grated

grated rind and juice of 1 lime

pinch of grated nutmeg

salt and pepper

Topping:

2 tablespoons oil

1 small onion, chopped

1 garlic clove, crushed

1 red chilli, deseeded and chopped

1 tablespoon chopped coriander

4 tablespoons fish stock

Oven temperature: 180°C (350°F), Gas Mark 4

1   To make the stuffing, put the breadcrumbs into a bowl and mix in the melted butter, then all the remaining ingredients. Blend well, cover and set aside.

2   Wash and dry the fish fillets and place in a large dish. Sprinkle with the lime juice and season inside and out with salt and pepper. Set aside in a cool place for about 1 hour to marinate.

3   To make the topping, heat the oil in a frying pan and add the onion and garlic. Fry gently until the onion is softened and golden. Add the chilli and continue cooking for 2–3 minutes, then stir in the chopped coriander and fish stock.

4   Remove the fish fillets from the marinade and sandwich together with the stuffing. Fasten with skewers or wooden cocktail sticks. Pour over the oil and any remaining marinade, and scatter the topping mixture over the fish. Bake in a preheated oven, 180°C (350°F), Gas Mark 4, for 20 minutes. Serve garnished with deep-fried onion rings.

active

Laksa

An authentic Asian dish that is a meal in itself; a tantalizing coconut and chicken broth is poured over fresh noodles and finished with chopped spring onions, red chilli and roasted peanuts.

3 tablespoons groundnut oil

2 large onions, finely chopped

4 garlic cloves, crushed

3 red bird chillies, finely chopped

75 g (3 oz) roasted peanuts, chopped

1 tablespoon ground coriander

1 tablespoon ground cumin

2 teaspoons turmeric

1.2 litres (2 pints) coconut milk

1 teaspoon shrimp paste (optional)

1–2 tablespoons sugar, to taste

375 g (12 oz) cooked chicken, shredded

175 g (6 oz) bean sprouts

500 g (1 lb) fresh flat rice noodles

4 spring onions, chopped

3 tablespoons chopped coriander leaves

salt and pepper

To serve:

4 spring onions, chopped

1 large red chilli, finely sliced

1–2 tablespoons chopped roasted peanuts

1 Heat the oil and fry the onions until golden brown. Add the garlic, chillies, peanuts, ground coriander, cumin and turmeric and fry for 2–3 minutes or until the spices have cooked through and released a strong aroma.

2 Stir the coconut milk and shrimp paste, if using, into the spice mixture, cover the pan and leave to simmer for 15 minutes. Season the spiced coconut with salt, pepper and sugar to taste. Add the shredded chicken and half of the bean sprouts to the coconut mixture and simmer for 5 minutes.

3 Blanch the fresh noodles in boiling water and divide between 4 large warmed bowls. Sprinkle with the spring onions and chopped coriander and divide the remaining raw bean sprouts between the bowls.

4 Ladle the chicken and coconut mixture over the noodles and serve with chopped spring onions, sliced red chilli and roasted peanuts.

Stir-fried duck

In this modern recipe the sweet, juicy fruitiness of mango counteracts the richness of duck meat and tempers the fieriness of red hot chilli.

with mango

1 large boneless, duck breast (magret), weighing about
  400 g (13 oz) or 2 small duck breasts
1 ripe mango
4 tablespoons groundnut oil
1 large red chilli, sliced into very thin rings
4 tablespoons Chinese rice wine or dry sherry
75 g (3 oz) Chinese mustard greens (gai choy), torn or shredded

Marinade:

2 tablespoons light or dark soy sauce
1 tablespoon rice wine vinegar or white wine or cider vinegar
½ teaspoon chilli oil
2.5 cm (1 inch) piece fresh root ginger, peeled and grated
½ teaspoon Chinese five spice powder

1 Strip the skin and fat off the duck and discard. Cut
   the duck flesh into thin strips, working diagonally
   across the grain, then place them in a non-metallic
   dish. Mix together the marinade ingredients, pour
   them into the dish and stir to mix. Cover and leave
   to marinate at room temperature for about
   30 minutes.

2 Meanwhile, cut the mango lengthways into three
   pieces, avoiding the long central stone. Peel the
   pieces of mango and cut the flesh into strips about
   the same size as the duck strips.

3 Heat an empty wok until hot. Add half of the oil and
   heat until it is hot. Add half the duck and stir-fry over
   a high heat for 4–5 minutes or until just tender.
   Remove the duck with a slotted spoon and repeat
   with the remaining oil and duck.

4 Return all of the duck to the wok and sprinkle with
   the chilli and rice wine or sherry. Toss to mix, then
   add the mango and mustard greens and toss for
   1–2 minutes, just until the greens start to wilt.
   Serve immediately.

Get marinating, get squeezing and get flaming with these delicious pork kebabs, accompanied by a tart grapefruit salsa.

Pork and juniper kebabs with ruby grapefruit salsa

500 g (1 lb) pork fillet, trimmed and cut into
    4 cm (1½ inch) cubes
about 16 bay leaves

Marinade:

1 ruby grapefruit
2 tablespoons lime juice
3 tablespoons clear honey
2 garlic cloves, crushed
6 juniper berries, finely crushed
100 ml (3½ fl oz) walnut or olive oil

Salsa:

2 ruby grapefruit
2 tablespoons chopped chives
2 tablespoons very finely chopped red onion
salt and pepper

1   To make the marinade, squeeze the juice from the grapefruit, working over a bowl so that no juice is wasted. Stir the remaining marinade ingredients into the bowl of juice and mix well. Add the pork cubes, turn to coat thoroughly, then cover and leave to marinate for 1–2 hours.

2   To make the grapefruit salsa, chop the grapefruit segments and place them in a bowl. Stir in the chives and onion and season with salt and pepper then set aside.

3   Remove the meat from the marinade and thread on to 4 skewers, placing a bay leaf between each piece of meat.

4   Place the kebabs under a preheated moderate grill or on a barbecue and cook for 15–20 minutes, turning and basting frequently with the remaining marinade. Serve with the gràpefruit salsa.

Spicy beef koftas in pizzaiola sauce

52

Leap into action with these meatballs in a spicy sauce, in which fresh chilli and garlic play a starring role.

53

1 egg

50 g (2 oz) coarse breadcrumbs

500 g (1 lb) lean minced beef

75 g (3 oz) onion, grated

2 tablespoons flour

2 tablespoons sunflower or olive oil

salt and pepper

flat leaf parsley sprigs, to garnish

Pizzaiola Sauce:

1–2 tablespoons sunflower or olive oil

1 large onion, finely chopped

2 garlic cloves, crushed

1 red chilli, deseeded and finely chopped

1–2 red peppers, cored, deseeded and chopped

400 g (13 oz) can plum tomatoes

300 ml (½ pint) beef stock

2 tablespoons tomato purée

2 tablespoons finely chopped basil

1 teaspoon finely chopped oregano

1 tablespoon chopped flat leaf parsley

pinch of sugar

75 g (3 oz) black Kalamata olives, pitted

1 First make the koftas. Beat the egg in a large bowl, stir in the breadcrumbs and add the beef and onion. Season with salt and pepper. Work together until well combined. You will find that your hands are best for this. Divide the mixture into 8 portions, shape each one into a ball and roll in a little flour. Heat the oil in a large frying pan and fry the koftas until evenly browned, turning frequently. This will take about 10 minutes.

2 Meanwhile, prepare the sauce. Heat the oil in a saucepan and fry the onion and garlic until soft but not coloured. Add the remaining ingredients, except half of the olives. Bring to the boil and cook over a high heat for 10 minutes to concentrate the flavours and slightly reduce the liquid.

3 Using a slotted spoon, lower the koftas into the sauce. Cover and cook gently for about 30 minutes until the meat is cooked through and the sauce rich and pulpy. Remove about 50 ml (2 fl oz) of the sauce and a few olives and process to a thick purée in a food processor or blender. Stir back into the sauce. Taste and adjust the seasoning, if necessary, and garnish with the parsley sprigs and remaining olives before serving.

Pineapple with hazelnuts and crème fraîche

Pineapple works well on the griddle because of its high natural sugar content, which gives dramatic griddle pan lines.

1 pineapple, peeled, halved lengthways and sliced

125 g (4 oz) roasted hazelnuts, chopped

125 g (4 oz) crème fraîche

1   Heat a griddle pan or nonstick frying pan until hot.

2   Place the pineapple slices on the pan and cook for 1–2 minutes on each side until lightly caramelized.

3   Mix the hazelnuts into the crème fraîche and serve the griddled pineapple with the nutty crème fraîche spooned over it.

Banoffi pie

It's easy when you know how – just crumble, press and chill, then slice, toss and whip … and you've got an all-time favourite dessert.

250 g (8 oz) digestive biscuits
125 g (4 oz) butter

Filling:
175 g (6 oz) butter
175 g (6 oz) caster sugar
425 g (14 oz) can condensed milk

Topping:
2 bananas
1 tablespoon lemon juice
150 ml (¼ pint) whipping cream
25 g (1 oz) dark chocolate shavings

1   Crumble the digestive biscuits in a food processor or blender or place them between 2 sheets of grease-proof paper and crush with a rolling pin. Melt the butter in a saucepan and stir in the biscuit crumbs.

2   Press the biscuit mixture evenly over the base and sides of a deep 20 cm (8 inch) round flan tin. Chill until firm.

3   To make the filling, place the butter and sugar in a saucepan and heat gently. Once the butter has melted, stir gently. Stir in the condensed milk and bring slowly to the boil. Lower the heat and simmer for 5 minutes, stirring constantly, until the mixture becomes a caramel colour. Pour the filling over the prepared biscuit base and leave to cool, then chill until the mixture has set.

4   Slice the bananas and toss them in the lemon juice. Reserve one-quarter of the bananas for decoration and spread the rest over the filling. Whip the cream until thick and spread over the top. Decorate with the reserved banana slices and sprinkle with chocolate shavings.

Limeade

Preparation time 6 minutes + infusing & chilling **Serves** 4

Utilise your energy in a practical way and roll the limes around quite hard on a board with your hand before you cut them open to get as much juice as you can.

6 limes
125 g (4 oz) caster sugar
750 ml (1¼ pints) boiling water
pinch of salt
ice cubes
mint sprigs, to decorate

1 Halve the limes and squeeze the juice into a large jug. Put the shells into a heatproof bowl with the sugar and boiling water. Leave to infuse for 15 minutes.

2 Add the salt, give the infusion a good stir then strain it into the jug with the lime juice. Add half a dozen ice cubes, cover and refrigerate for 2 hours or until cold.

3 To serve, place 3–4 ice cubes in each glass and pour the limeade over them. Decorate each one with a sprig of mint.

Grapefruit mint cooler

59

Serve this pretty cocktail in old-fashioned glasses or tumblers with crushed ice and sprigs of mint – and drink to your heart's content.

125 g (4 oz) sugar
125 ml (4 fl oz) water
handful of mint
juice of 4 large lemons
450 ml (¾ pint) unsweetened grapefruit juice
crushed ice
250 ml (8 fl oz) soda water
mint sprigs, to decorate

1 Place the sugar and water in a heavy-based saucepan and stir over a low heat until the sugar has dissolved. Leave to cool. Crush the mint leaves and stir them into the syrup. Leave to stand for about 12 hours, then strain.

2 Add the lemon and grapefruit juices to the strained syrup and stir well. Fill 6 glasses with crushed ice and pour the cocktail into the glasses. Add the soda water then decorate each glass with a mint sprig.

Variation:
Cranberry Mint Cooler

Substitute cranberry juice for the grapefruit juice and prepare as in the main recipe.

Relaxed

Sometimes you simply have to cook a meal, but you don't want to spend hours in the kitchen when you'd far rather put your feet up and unwind. These quick and easy dishes should have you in and out of the kitchen in a matter of minutes, allowing you to spend your valuable time savouring a delicious meal on the sofa or in your favourite armchair. Each of these recipes has been specially designed to leave the dinner table out of the equation, be it a one-bowl meal to be eaten with chopsticks or a dish that lends itself perfectly to being eaten with your fingers. So unwind, relax, and bon appétit!

Starters and snacks

Main courses

Desserts

Drinks

Grilled radicchio and fontina bruschetta with anchovy relish

It's not just easy – it's so quick that if you blink and make yourself a cocktail, you won't even remember preparing it!

1 small radicchio head

125 g (4 oz) Fontina cheese

2–3 tablespoons olive oil

4 slices of rustic Italian bread, preferably one day old

1 garlic clove, peeled but left whole

2 tablespoons anchovy relish, such as Gentleman's Relish (Patum Peperium), or to taste

salt and pepper

Parmesan cheese shavings, to serve

1 Trim the radicchio, discarding any discoloured leaves. Cut it lengthways into quarters, wash and leave to dry. Cut the Fontina into thin slices and slip them in between the leaves of the radicchio.

2 Heat half the oil in a large frying pan, add the radicchio and fry gently for 2–3 minutes, then carefully turn and cook for a further 2 minutes until the radicchio is golden and the cheese has melted.

3 Meanwhile, grill or toast the bread on both sides and rub all over with the garlic clove, drizzle with a little oil and spread each one with anchovy relish. Season with salt and pepper.

4 Top the bruschetta with the radicchio, scatter over the Parmesan and serve immediately.

Braised chive flowers with prawns

The South-east Asians know a thing or two about flavour and it need not take ages to achieve – just 10–15 minutes.

1 tablespoon groundnut oil

2 garlic cloves, crushed

175 g (6 oz) flowering chives, large chives or spring onions, cut into 7 cm (3 inch) lengths

1 tablespoon Thai fish sauce

3 tablespoons dark soy sauce

2 teaspoons caster sugar

250 g (8 oz) raw prawns, peeled and roughly chopped

red chillies, sliced, to garnish

Thai jasmine rice, to serve (optional)

1 Heat the oil in a wok or large frying pan, add the garlic and stir-fry for 1 minute. Add the chives or spring onions, fish sauce, soy sauce and sugar and stir-fry for 1 further minute.

2 Add the raw prawns to the wok and stir-fry for 3 minutes until pink and cooked through. Serve immediately, garnished with red chillies. Thai jasmine rice makes a good accompaniment.

Butternut squash risotto

There's something surprisingly therapeutic about stirring a risotto, and this one tastes especially good.

66

1 butternut squash, weighing 1 kg (2 lb)
3 tablespoons olive oil
1 litre (1¾ pints) chicken or vegetable stock
125 g (4 oz) butter
1 garlic clove, chopped
1 onion, finely diced
300 g (10 oz) arborio or carnaroli rice
150 g (5 oz) Parmesan cheese, grated
salt and pepper
pumpkin seed oil, to serve (optional)

Oven temperature: 220°C (425°F), Gas Mark 7

1 Top and tail the squash, cut in half round the middle, then pare away the skin from the larger half without losing too much of the flesh. Cut in half lengthways, remove the seeds and cut into 5 cm (2 inch) dice. Repeat with the other half. Place on a large baking sheet, drizzle with 2 tablespoons of the olive oil and season with salt and pepper. Mix well and cook at the top of a preheated oven, 220°C (425°F), Gas Mark 7, for 15 minutes. The squash should be soft and lightly browned.

2 Meanwhile, heat the stock in a saucepan to a gentle simmer.

3 Melt the remaining olive oil and half the butter in a heavy-based saucepan, add the garlic and onion and sauté gently for 5 minutes; do not brown.

4 Add the rice, stir well to coat the grains with oil and butter, then add enough stock to cover the rice. Stir well and simmer gently. Continue to stir as frequently as possible throughout cooking. As the liquid is absorbed, continue adding ladlefuls of stock to just cover the rice. Continue to cook until all of the stock has been absorbed and the rice is just tender.

5 Remove the squash from the oven, add to the risotto with the Parmesan and the remaining butter, season with salt and pepper and stir gently.

6 Serve the risotto on individual warmed plates with a little pumpkin seed oil drizzled on top of each portion, if liked.

Chickpea and

This unusual variation of the classic tortilla is as effortless to prepare as it is delicious to eat.

6 tablespoons extra virgin olive oil

1 onion, chopped

4 garlic cloves, crushed

½ teaspoon crushed chilli flakes

500 g (1 lb) chard leaves

400 g (13 oz) can chickpeas, drained

6 eggs, beaten

2 tablespoons chopped parsley

salt and pepper

chard tortilla

1 Heat 4 tablespoons of the oil in a large, heavy-based frying pan. Add the onion, garlic and chilli flakes and fry gently for 10 minutes until softened and lightly golden.

2 Meanwhile, wash and dry the chard and cut away and discard the thick central white stem. Shred the leaves. Stir the chard into the onion mixture with the chickpeas and cook gently for 5 minutes.

3 Beat the eggs in a bowl, add the parsley and season with salt and pepper. Stir in the chickpea mixture.

4 Wipe out the pan, then add the remaining oil. Pour in the egg and chickpea mixture and cook over a low heat for 10 minutes until the tortilla is almost cooked through.

5 Carefully slide the tortilla out on to a large plate, invert the pan over the tortilla and then flip it back into the pan.

6 Return the pan to the heat and continue to cook for a further 5 minutes until cooked through. Allow to cool and serve cut into squares. Eat with your fingers.

Vegetable fajitas

Quick and easy, these are just the thing to pile on to a plate and eat over a napkin on the sofa.

2 tablespoons olive oil

2 large onions, thinly sliced

2 garlic cloves, crushed

2 red peppers, cored, deseeded and thinly sliced

2 green peppers, cored, deseeded and thinly sliced

4 green chillies, deseeded and thinly sliced

2 teaspoons chopped oregano

250 g (8 oz) button mushrooms, sliced

salt and pepper

To serve:

12 warmed tortillas

chives

1　Heat the olive oil in a large frying pan and gently sauté the onions and garlic for about 5 minutes until they are soft and golden brown.

2　Add the red and green peppers, chillies and oregano and stir well. Sauté gently for about 10 minutes, until cooked and tender.

3　Add the button mushrooms and cook quickly for 1 minute more, stirring to mix the mushrooms thoroughly with the other vegetables. Season the vegetable mixture with salt and pepper to taste.

4　To serve, spoon the sizzling hot vegetable mixture into the warmed tortillas and roll up or fold over. Serve hot, with chives.

Baby vegetable stir-fry with orange and oyster sauce

72

Ready in a flash of the pan,
it's hard to believe that
something as full of flavour
can be so quick to make.

2 tablespoons groundnut oil

175 g (6 oz) baby carrots

175 g (6 oz) baby sweetcorn

175 g (6 oz) small button mushrooms

salt and pepper

coriander leaves, to garnish

egg noodles, to serve

Orange and oyster sauce:

2 teaspoons cornflour

4 tablespoons cold water

finely grated rind and juice of 1 large orange

2 tablespoons oyster sauce

1 tablespoon rice wine or dry sherry

1   First prepare the sauce. Blend the cornflour in a jug
    with the cold water, then add the orange rind and
    juice, the oyster sauce and rice wine or sherry. Stir
    well to combine.

2   Heat an empty wok until hot. Add the oil and heat
    again. Add the carrots and sweetcorn and stir-fry for
    5 minutes, then add the mushrooms and stir-fry for
    3–4 minutes more.

3   Pour in the sauce mixture and bring to the boil over
    a high heat, stirring constantly until thickened and
    glossy. Add salt and pepper to taste. Garnish with
    coriander leaves and serve with egg noodles.

These open sandwiches are great made with fresh tuna and served on a summer's evening as a quick supper dish with a glass of chilled white wine.

Tuna steak sandwich with spinach, ricotta and olive filling

75 g (3 oz) pitted olives
1 garlic clove, crushed
1 bunch of basil
1 tablespoon balsamic vinegar
3 tablespoons olive oil
4 x 175 g (6 oz) tuna steaks
4 slices of granary or rye bread
125 g (4 oz) ricotta cheese
1 small bag of baby spinach leaves
salt and pepper
lemon wedges, to serve

1   Heat a griddle pan or nonstick frying pan until it is very hot.

2   Place the olives, garlic, basil, vinegar and olive oil in a food processor or blender and process. Alternatively, chop by hand and mix together.

3   Put the tuna steaks on the hot griddle or in the frying pan and cook for 1–2 minutes on each side.

4   Toast the bread, spread each slice with ricotta, top with generous amounts of spinach and season well. Place a tuna steak on top of each sandwich and spoon over the green sauce and serve with lemon wedges.

Preparation time 10 minutes Cooking time 8 minutes Serves 4

In the time it takes to cook the pasta, you can assemble a delicious sauce to go with it, which will literally melt in the mouth.

Fettuccine with smoked salmon and asparagus sauce

375 g (12 oz) fettuccine
175 g (6 oz) asparagus tips
125 g (4 oz) smoked salmon, cut into thin strips
300 ml (½ pint) double cream
1 tablespoon tarragon leaves
salt and pepper
Parmesan cheese shavings, to garnish (optional)

1 Cook the fettuccine in lightly salted boiling water for 8–12 minutes, or according to packet instructions, until just tender. Drain and return to the pan. Meanwhile, blanch the asparagus tips in boiling water for 5 minutes, drain under cold running water and pat dry.

2 Toss the pasta over a low heat with the asparagus, smoked salmon, cream, tarragon and salt and pepper to taste, until heated through.

3 Transfer to a warmed serving dish and garnish with wafer-thin shavings of Parmesan cheese, if liked.

Variation:
Smoked Salmon and Mushroom Sauce

Use 375 g (12 oz) mixed ceps, shiitake and oyster mushrooms instead of the asparagus. Cut into even-sized pieces and stir-fry in 2 tablespoons olive oil for 5–7 minutes, then add to the pasta as above.

Have everything you need prepared before you start to cook, and you'll be amazed at how quickly this dish is ready.

Chicken with vegetables, noodles and cashew nuts

50 ml (2 fl oz) sunflower oil

1 tablespoon light sesame seed oil

750 g (1½ lb) boneless, skinless chicken breast, cut into thin strips

1 large carrot, cut into thin strips

2 large peppers, cored, deseeded and cut into thin strips

175 g (6 oz) mangetout

175 g (6 oz) baby sweetcorn

375 g (12 oz) medium egg noodles, cooked and drained

75 g (3 oz) cashew nuts, toasted

2 spring onions, thinly sliced

coriander leaves, to garnish

Sauce:

1½ tablespoons cornflour

3 garlic cloves, finely chopped

2 teaspoons finely grated fresh root ginger

3 tablespoons dark soft brown sugar

6 tablespoons tamari sauce

1 teaspoon Tabasco sauce

450 ml (¾ pint) chicken stock

1 First combine all the ingredients for the sauce in a jug, gradually adding the stock to make a smooth liquid.

2 Combine the sunflower and sesame oils, heat half the mixture in a wok or large frying pan and stir-fry the chicken strips until cooked. This will only take about 3 minutes. Remove from the pan. Add the remaining oil mixture and stir-fry the carrot for 1 minute, then add the peppers, mangetout and sweetcorn, constantly tossing and frying over a high heat.

3 Stir the sauce to make sure it is well blended, then pour it into the pan. Bring to the boil and cook for a few minutes, stirring all the time, to thicken. Add the noodles and chicken and cook for a further few minutes to heat thoroughly.

4 Pile a generous helping in the centre of each of 4 warmed bowls and sprinkle over the cashew nuts, spring onions and a little of the sauce. Garnish with coriander and serve immediately.

Thai cooking has a lot to offer in terms of rapid and flavourful meals that you can eat in a bowl with nothing more than a pair of chopsticks.

Fried rice with pork and mushrooms

3 tablespoons oil

100 g (3½ oz) pork, cut into bite-sized pieces

1 garlic clove, chopped

1 egg

375 g (12 oz) cold cooked rice

1 tomato, cut into 8 pieces

1 teaspoon palm sugar or light muscovado sugar

3 tablespoons Thai fish sauce

65 g (2½ oz) oyster mushrooms, sliced

15 g (½ oz) spring onion, diagonally sliced

coriander leaves, to garnish

1 Heat the oil in a wok, add the pork and garlic and stir-fry for 2–3 minutes until they begin to turn golden. Break the egg into the wok and stir it around well.

2 Add the rice and stir-fry for 2–3 minutes, then add the tomato and sugar and stir-fry for 1 minute. Add the fish sauce and stir, then add the mushrooms and stir-fry for 1 minute.

3 Finally add the spring onion and mix thoroughly. Turn the rice into a bowl and serve, garnished with the coriander leaves.

Bananas in coconut milk

This oh-so-yummy dessert is simplicity itself, and quicker to prepare than the time it takes to say coconut milk!

200 ml (7 fl oz) coconut milk

100 ml (3½ fl oz) water

3 tablespoons palm sugar or light muscovado sugar

1 large or 2 small bananas, diagonally sliced

rose petals, to decorate (optional)

1   Put the coconut milk, water and sugar into a saucepan and simmer, stirring occasionally, for about 6 minutes.

2   Add the bananas and cook for 4 minutes until heated through. Decorate with rose petals, if liked, and serve hot.

83

Chocolate
mousse

Incredibly rich, amazingly quick, unbelievably naughty, and utterly delicious – sheer bliss! There's nothing like it.

4 eggs, separated
125 g (4 oz) caster sugar
125 g (4 oz) plain chocolate, broken into pieces
3 tablespoons water
300 ml (½ pint) double cream

To serve:
65 ml (2½ fl oz) whipping cream, whipped to
  firm peaks
chocolate shavings

1   Put the egg yolks and sugar into a bowl and whisk with an electric beater until thick and mousse-like.

2   Melt the chocolate with the water in a heatproof bowl set over a pan of simmering water. Remove from the heat and let cool slightly, then whisk into the egg mixture.

3   Whip the double cream until it stands in soft peaks, then carefully fold into the chocolate mixture.

4   Whisk the egg whites until stiff, carefully fold 1 tablespoon into the mousse, and then fold in the rest. Pour into 4–6 cups or small dishes and chill until set.

5   To serve, top each mousse with whipped cream, then sprinkle over the chocolate shavings.

Variation: Chocolate Orange Mousse

Follow step 1 of the main recipe; then whisk the finely grated rind of 1 orange and 1 tablespoon of Cointreau into the mousse-like mixture. Proceed as for the main recipe.

Mint tea

Preparation time 10 minutes **Serves** 4

Serve hot or iced, and enjoy the refreshing flavour of this fragrant sweet tea – just the thing to relax you after a hard day.

2 teaspoons Chinese green tea
4 tablespoons chopped mint, preferably spearmint
900 ml (1½ pints) water
sugar, to taste

To decorate:
4 lemon slices (optional)
4 small mint sprigs

1 Rinse a teapot with boiling water. Add the tea and mint to the pot. Bring the water to the boil and immediately pour into the teapot. Leave to stand for 5 minutes.

2 Pour the tea through a strainer into warmed heat-proof glasses or small cups. Add sugar to taste and decorate each glass or cup with a lemon slice, if liked, and a sprig of mint.

Variation: Iced Mint Tea

Add the sugar to the pot with the tea and mint. After steeping, pour the tea through a strainer over cracked ice so it cools quickly. Serve in cold glasses with ice cubes, decorated in the same way.

Preparation time 5 minutes **Serves** 2–3

Iced strawberry and banana shake

87

A sure winner with children, but there's a child in all of us and many are the adults who will enjoy this.

250 g (8 oz) strawberries, hulled and halved

1 small banana, sliced

1 scoop strawberry sorbet

2 scoops vanilla ice cream

100 ml (3½ fl oz) milk, chilled

whipped cream, to serve (optional)

strawberry halves, to decorate

1 Put the strawberries, banana, sorbet, ice cream and milk into a food processor or blender and process until smooth. Add more ice cream for a thicker shake, or more milk for a thinner drink, if you like. Serve in tall glasses, topped with whipped cream, if liked, and decorated with strawberry halves.

ld

Some days you may be perfectly happy to cook up those old stand-bys, things you can rely on to be quick and easy, like a simple pasta dish or a time-honoured baked potato. But there are bound to be times when you want to strike out, to be adventurous and try something out of the ordinary. Perhaps you've invited someone special over to dinner and you want to impress, or maybe you are tempted by a new idea, something you've never attempted before. When the mood takes you, the old tried and tested recipes just won't do. That is the time to be a daredevil, to throw caution to the wind and to dive into this chapter. Spice up your mealtimes with this fantastic collision of flavours from all over the world.

Starters and snacks

Main courses

Desserts

Drinks

Pork ball and

Take a walk on the wild side
and try this unusual soup – it
packs an unexpected punch.

3 dried black fungi
50 g (2 oz) rice vermicelli
600 ml (1 pint) chicken stock
2 garlic cloves, sliced
100 g (3½ oz) minced pork
2 tablespoons light soy sauce
1 tablespoon Thai fish sauce

1   Soak the fungi in warm water for 30 minutes, then drain
    and slice. Soak the rice vermicelli in warm water for
    20 minutes, then drain and cut into 5 cm (2 inch) lengths.

2   Heat the stock and add the garlic.

3   Shape the pork into little round balls. Drop them into the
    stock and simmer for 5 minutes.

4   Add the black fungi, soy sauce, fish sauce and rice
    vermicelli, cook for about 2 minutes and serve.

black fungus soup

Steamboat soup

Tiger prawns, squid and trout jostle for space in this fabulous seafood soup from faraway Cambodia. Serve in a steamboat or fondue pot, if possible, so the soup finishes cooking at the table.

8 tablespoons vegetable oil

1 garlic clove, thinly sliced

1 tablespoon tamarind pulp

150 ml (¼ pint) boiling water

1.2 litres (2 pints) cold water

2 tablespoons Thai fish sauce

1 teaspoon caster sugar

1 small pineapple, peeled, cored and cut into chunks

175 g (6 oz) tomatoes, quartered

8 spring onions, finely sliced

250 g (8 oz) raw tiger prawns, peeled

3 small squid, cleaned and cut into thick rings

250 g (8 oz) rainbow trout fillets, cut into pieces

To serve:

handful of coriander leaves

handful of sweet basil leaves

2 large chillies, diagonally sliced

1   Heat the vegetable oil in a small saucepan. When it is hot, deep-fry the garlic, a few slices at a time, until golden brown. Remove the garlic and drain on kitchen paper.

2   Put the tamarind pulp in a bowl with the boiling water and set aside for 20 minutes to soften. Strain the liquid through a sieve (discarding the pods and tamarind stones) and place in a pan with the cold water, fish sauce, caster sugar, pineapple chunks, tomatoes and spring onions. Slowly bring to the boil.

3   If you are using a steamboat or fondue pot, pour the flavoured stock into the hot pan over smoking coals or a flame and add the tiger prawns, squid rings and pieces of fish. Simmer gently for 6–8 minutes.

4   Serve the steamboat while the fish is cooking. Top with coriander and basil leaves, slices of chilli and the deep-fried garlic.

Steamed wontons

Wontons, filled with prawns, pork and water chestnuts, are the perfect Oriental fast food – short on labour, high on flavour.

1 To make the filling, blend all the ingredients in a food processor or blender.

2 Put 1 heaped teaspoon of the filling into the centre of a wonton wrapper, placed on the side of your hand over your thumb and index finger. As you push the filled wrapper down through the circle your fingers form, tighten the top, shaping it but leaving the top open. Repeat this process with all the wrappers.

3 Put the filled wontons on to a plate and place the plate in a steamer. Drizzle a little oil on top of the wontons, put the lid on and steam for 30 minutes.

4 Serve the wontons hot or warm, with soy sauce and chilli sauce for dipping.

16 wonton wrappers
a little oil

Filling:
6 raw prawns, peeled
125 g (4 oz) minced pork
40 g (1½ oz) onion, finely chopped
2 garlic cloves
5 water chestnuts
1 teaspoon palm sugar or light muscovado sugar
1 tablespoon light soy sauce
1 egg

To serve:
soy sauce
chilli sauce

Briks

Originally from North Africa, briks (pronounced breeks) should be eaten piping hot, crisp and golden.

about 250 g (8 oz) filo pastry, thawed if frozen
olive oil, for brushing
sesame seeds, for sprinkling

Filling:

50 g (2 oz) olives, pitted
3 anchovy fillets
3 sun-dried tomatoes in oil, drained and
  chopped
2 tablespoons chopped almonds
2 tablespoons chopped mixed coriander
  and parsley
3 soft-boiled eggs, chopped
lemon juice, to taste
pepper

Oven temperature: 190°C (375°F), Gas Mark 5

1 To make the filling, finely chop the olives and anchovy fillets together, then mix them with the tomatoes, almonds, herbs, eggs and lemon juice, and season with pepper.

2 Cut the pastry into eight 25 cm (4 x 10 inch) strips. Work with 3–4 strips at a time, keeping the remaining pastry covered with clingfilm or a damp tea towel to prevent it drying out.

3 Brush the strips lightly with oil and place a heaped teaspoon of the filling at the top right-hand corner of each one. Fold the corner over the filling to make a triangle. Continue folding the triangle over and over along the length of the strip of pastry. Place on a baking sheet and brush with oil. Repeat until all the filling has been used.

4 Sprinkle the briks with sesame seeds and bake in a preheated oven, 190°C (375°F), Gas Mark 5, for about 20 minutes until crisp and golden. Serve hot.

Chimichangas

A classic Mexican dish, chimichangas are vegetable tortillas with more than a hint of chilli.

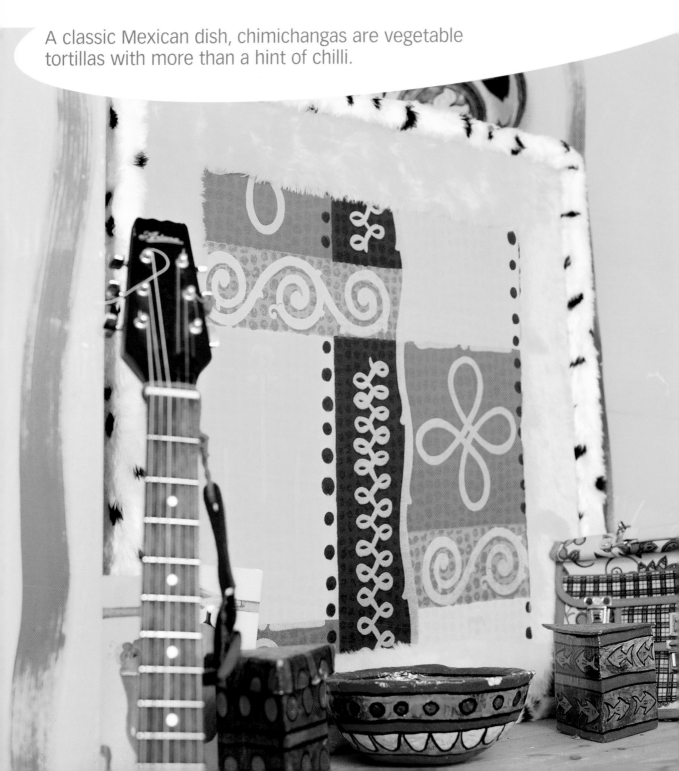

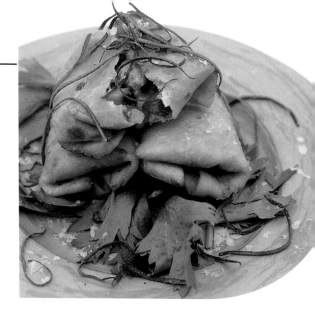

2 tablespoons olive oil

1 small onion, chopped

1 red pepper, cored, deseeded and diced

125 g (4 oz) button mushrooms, thinly sliced

2 tomatoes, skinned, deseeded and chopped

2 red chillies, deseeded and finely chopped

175 g (6 oz) Cheddar cheese, grated

8 wheat flour tortillas

oil, for deep-frying

sea salt and pepper

coriander sprigs, to serve

skin of 2 courgettes, very thinly sliced into strips, to garnish

1 Heat the olive oil in a heavy-based frying pan, add the onion and red pepper and sauté until just tender but still slightly crisp. Add the mushrooms, tomatoes and chillies and stir-fry over a medium heat for 3–4 minutes. Season to taste with sea salt and pepper.

2 Remove the frying pan from the heat and mix the grated Cheddar cheese into the vegetable mixture. Stir gently until the cheese melts.

3 Divide the vegetable and cheese mixture into 8 portions and put one in the centre of each of the tortillas. Carefully fold the two opposite sides of the tortillas over the filling, then fold the loose edges under so that the parcel is completely sealed.

4 Heat the oil for deep-frying in a heavy-based frying pan and fry the tortillas, 1–2 at a time, in the hot oil until crisp and golden, turning once during cooking. Remove from the oil with a slotted spoon and drain on kitchen paper, keeping the tortillas warm while frying the remaining batches. Serve on a bed of coriander, garnished with courgette strips and sprinkled with salt.

Variation: Broccoli chimichangas

Make the chimichangas as in the main recipe, adding 250 g (8 oz) small steamed broccoli florets to the vegetable mixture, then continue as in the main recipe. Serve with guacamole and soured cream.

Black bean kebabs with mango relish

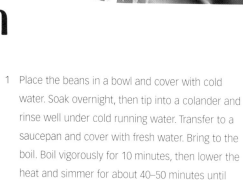

These take a little time to make, but they're worth every last second, as we're sure you'll agree.

125 g (4 oz) dried black beans
3 tablespoons olive oil
1 onion, very finely chopped
1 garlic clove, crushed
1 red chilli, deseeded and finely chopped
1 teaspoon ground coriander
1 tablespoon chopped fresh coriander
2 courgettes
24 mixed red and yellow cherry tomatoes
rice, to serve

Mango relish:

1 ripe mango, peeled and stoned
1 small onion, grated
1 red chilli, deseeded and finely chopped
1 cm (½ inch) piece of fresh root ginger, peeled and grated
salt and pepper

1 Place the beans in a bowl and cover with cold water. Soak overnight, then tip into a colander and rinse well under cold running water. Transfer to a saucepan and cover with fresh water. Bring to the boil. Boil vigorously for 10 minutes, then lower the heat and simmer for about 40–50 minutes until tender. Drain well and set the beans aside.

2 To make the mango relish, place the mango flesh in a bowl and mash lightly. Add the onion, chilli and ginger and mix well. Season with a little salt and pepper and set aside.

3 Heat 2 tablespoons of the oil in pan. Add the onion, garlic and chilli and cook for 5–10 minutes until the onion is soft. Add the ground coriander and cook for 1–2 minutes more. Turn the onion and spice mixture into a bowl, add the drained beans and fresh coriander and mash well. Form the mixture into 24 balls.

4 Cut the courgettes lengthways into thin ribbons and brush with the remaining oil. Thread the bean balls on metal skewers alternating with the cherry tomatoes and weaving the courgette strips in between. Cook the kebabs under a preheated moderate grill or on a barbecue over moderately hot coals for 4 minutes on each side. Serve with the mango relish and plain boiled rice.

Stir-fried squid with basil

This is a simple but sizzlingly-hot stir-fry, aimed at those who are sure that they can stand the heat in the kitchen.

Crispy shallots:

500 ml (1 pint) groundnut oil

25 g (1 oz) shallots, finely chopped

2 tablespoons oil

6 garlic cloves, chopped

12 small green chillies, finely sliced

1–2 shallots, chopped

125 g (4 oz) squid, cleaned, cut into strips and scored in a criss-cross fashion

½ green pepper, cored, deseeded and chopped

2 tablespoons fish stock

1 tablespoon Thai fish sauce

1 teaspoon palm sugar or light muscovado sugar

15 g (½ oz) basil leaves

1   First make the crispy shallots for the garnish. Heat the oil for deep-frying in a wok or deep saucepan. When it is really hot, add the shallots and stir for 1½–2 minutes until golden. Remove with a slotted spoon and drain on kitchen paper. When the oil is cold, it can be returned to an airtight container to use another time.

2   Heat the oil in a wok, add the garlic, chillies and shallots and fry for 30 seconds.

3   Add the squid and green pepper, turn the heat to high and stir-fry for 1 minute then reduce the heat and add the stock, fish sauce, sugar and basil. Cook, stirring, for 1 minute, then serve, garnished with the crispy shallots.

Crisp fried fish with chilli and basil

3 garlic cloves, thinly sliced

2 coriander roots, finely chopped

2 fresh red chillies, finely chopped

1 dried red chilli, finely chopped

3 teaspoons caster sugar

1 tablespoon oil, plus extra for deep-frying

3 tablespoons Thai fish sauce

3 tablespoons soy sauce

3 kaffir lime leaves, finely shredded

5 tablespoons fish stock or water

500 g (1 lb) catfish, sea bass or cod, filleted
   and cubed

To serve:

20–30 holy basil leaves

1 fresh red chilli, shredded

A firm-fleshed white fish is deep-fried Thai-style with plenty of chilli to liven things up.

1 Blend the garlic, coriander roots, fresh and dried chillies and sugar in a food processor or pound to a paste using a pestle and mortar.

2 Heat the tablespoon of oil in a wok or frying pan and stir-fry the chilli paste for 1–2 minutes. Add the fish sauce, soy sauce and lime leaves and stir-fry for 1 minute then add the stock or water and bring to a fast boil. Continue boiling until the sauce has reduced a little.

3 Heat the oil for deep-frying in a saucepan and, when it is hot, add the pieces of fish and fry until crisp and golden brown. Remove the fish from the oil with a slotted spoon, add to the chilli sauce and toss together.

4 Deep-fry the basil leaves for 30 seconds, remove and drain on kitchen paper. Serve the fish topped with the deep-fried basil and shreds of red chilli.

Sail away on an adventure of taste and discovery with this aromatic Vietnamese dish of fish wrapped in banana leaves.

Sizzling fish in banana

4 large squares of banana leaf

4 x 175 g (6 oz) swordfish, snapper or sea bass fillets, 2.5 cm (1 inch) thick

Spice paste:

1 lemon grass stalk, very finely chopped

2 large garlic cloves, finely chopped

1 kaffir lime leaf, finely shredded

2 shallots, finely chopped

125 g (4 oz) butter

2 teaspoons lime juice

1 tablespoon finely chopped coriander leaves

1 green chilli, finely chopped

1 red chilli, finely chopped

salt and pepper

To serve:

boiled rice

stir-fried green vegetable

1 First make the spice paste. Blend the lemon grass, garlic, kaffir lime leaf and shallots to a smooth paste in a food processor or with a pestle and mortar. Add the butter, lime juice, coriander and green and red chillies, then season to taste with salt and pepper and blend again.

2 Put the banana leaves into a bowl, pour boiling water over them, then drain; this makes them easier to bend and wrap. Place a fish fillet in the centre of each leaf and cover it with some of the spice paste. Wrap it up into a tight parcel and secure with a bamboo skewer or cocktail stick.

3 Chill the fish parcels in the refrigerator until you are ready to cook. Cook under a preheated hot grill or on a barbecue for 8–10 minutes, turning once. Serve the fish still wrapped in the banana leaves. Cut open the parcels and the aromatic, buttery fish awaits. Eat with boiled rice and a stir-fried green vegetable.

eaves

Tender cubes of lamb cooked
with okra and almonds are an
unusual combination of flavours,
surely made in heaven.

Lamb tagine with okra and almonds

1 kg (2 lb) boneless shoulder or leg of lamb, cut into
   large cubes

1 onion, chopped

3 garlic cloves, crushed

1 large red pepper, cored, deseeded and sliced

5 cm (2 inch) piece of fresh root ginger, peeled and grated

2 teaspoons ground cinnamon

2 teaspoons paprika

600 ml (1 pint) vegetable stock or water

1½ tablespoons clear honey

4 tablespoons lemon juice

375 g (12 oz) okra, trimmed

75 g (3 oz) whole blanched almonds

salt and pepper

1 Put the lamb, onion, garlic, red pepper, ginger,
   cinnamon, paprika, stock, honey and lemon juice
   into a heavy flameproof casserole and heat to just
   on simmering point. Cover the casserole tightly and
   cook for 1¼ hours, stirring occasionally.

2 Add the okra and almonds to the tagine. Cover the
   casserole or leave it uncovered if there is a lot of
   liquid left, and cook for a further 15–20 minutes until
   the okra is tender.

3 Season to taste with salt and pepper and serve.

Beef kebabs with beetroot and horseradish salsa

A hot beetroot and horseradish salsa is sure to make your kebabs a memorable feast.

750 g (1½ lb) sirloin steak, trimmed and cut into 16 long
   thin strips
8 long, woody rosemary sprigs
4 tablespoons balsamic vinegar
175 ml (6 fl oz) red wine
4 tablespoons olive oil
1 tablespoon cracked black pepper
salt

Beetroot and horseradish salsa:
250 g (8 oz) cooked beetroot, peeled and chopped
½ red onion, finely chopped
1–2 tablespoons finely grated fresh horseradish or
   creamed horseradish
salt and pepper

1 Thread 2 pieces of steak on to each sprig of
rosemary, concertina fashion, and place in a shallow
dish. Mix together the vinegar, wine, olive oil and
pepper and pour over the steak. Turn to coat
thoroughly, then cover and leave to marinate for
1–2 hours.

2 To make the salsa, mix the beetroot, onion and
horseradish, season with salt and pepper and
set aside.

3 Remove the kebabs from the marinade and sprinkle
with a little salt. Cook under a preheated hot grill or
on a barbecue for 3–4 minutes on each side, basting
frequently with the remaining marinade. Serve with
the salsa.

Indian pistachio and
112
saffron ice creams

125 g (4 oz) caster sugar

3 cardamom pods, bruised

900 ml (1½ pints) evaporated milk

150 ml (¼ pint) double cream

75 g (3 oz) pistachio nuts, finely chopped

20 saffron threads, soaked overnight in
  4 tablespoons hot milk

edible gold or silver leaf, to decorate (optional)

1 Put the sugar and cardamoms in a heavy-based saucepan with the evaporated milk and the cream and simmer very gently for 10 minutes. Divide the milk mixture between 2 jugs and add pistachio nuts to one and the saffron and milk mixture to the other. Set aside to cool.

2 Pour the mixture into small kulfi or other ice cream moulds and freeze until solid. To serve, turn out on to small dessert plates and decorate with small pieces of gold or silver leaf, if using.

Flaming lamborghini

Preparation time 8 minutes **Serves** 1

A flaming cocktail mixture to set your spirit alight and enhance even the wildest of moods.

1 measure Kahlúa

1 measure Sambuca

1 measure Bailey's Irish Cream

1 measure blue Curaçao

1   Pour the Kahlúa into a warmed cocktail glass. Gently pour half a measure of Sambuca over the back of a spoon into the cocktail glass to create two layers.

2   Pour the Bailey's and blue Curaçao into a short glass.

3   Pour the remaining Sambuca into a warmed wine glass and carefully set the Sambuca alight with a match. Pour into the cocktail glass with care.

4   Pour the Bailey's and Curaçao into the flaming cocktail glass. Drink with a straw and enjoy.

Astronaut

Mix rum and vodka with
lemon and passion fruit
juices, then drink slowly
and head for the stars.

8–10 ice cubes

½ measure white rum

½ measure vodka

½ measure fresh lemon juice

1 dash passion fruit juice

lemon wedge, to decorate

1 Put 4–5 ice cubes into a cocktail shaker and add the
rum, vodka, lemon and passion fruit juices. Fill an
old-fashioned glass with the remaining ice cubes.
Shake the drink then strain it into the glass. Decorate
with the lemon wedge and serve.

ROMANTIC

Starters and snacks

Main courses

Desserts

Drinks

The link between food and romance has been made by poets and authors since time immemorial. Certain ingredients are well known for their aphrodisiac qualities, such as seafood, asparagus and chocolate to name but three, and there are ideas in this chapter for all of them. When you are creating a romantic meal for two, you will want to spend more time enjoying each other's company than cooking alone in the kitchen, and all these recipes have been designed with this in mind. There are some more extravagant dishes that are suited to a candle-lit dinner *à deux*, while others are more suitable for sharing on the sofa together during a quiet evening at home.

Mexican soup with avocado salsa

1 tablespoon sunflower oil

1 small onion, chopped

1 garlic clove, crushed

1 teaspoon ground coriander

½ teaspoon ground cumin

½ red pepper, cored, deseeded and diced

1 red chilli, deseeded and sliced

200 g (7 oz) canned red kidney beans, drained

375 ml (13 fl oz) tomato juice

1 tablespoon chilli sauce

15 g (½ oz) tortilla chips, crushed

salt and pepper

coriander sprigs, to garnish

Avocado salsa:

1 small ripe avocado

4 spring onions, finely chopped

1 tablespoon lemon juice

1 tablespoon chopped coriander

1 Heat the oil in a large, heavy-based saucepan, add the onion, garlic, spices, red pepper and two-thirds of the chilli and fry gently for 10 minutes. Add the kidney beans, tomato juice and chilli sauce, bring to the boil, cover and simmer gently for 30 minutes.

2 Meanwhile, make the avocado salsa. Peel, stone and finely dice the avocado, put into a bowl and combine it with the spring onions, lemon juice and coriander. Season with salt and pepper to taste, cover with clingfilm and set aside.

3 Process the soup in a food processor or blender, together with the crushed tortilla chips. Return the soup to a clean saucepan, season to taste with salt and pepper and heat through. Serve the soup immediately with the avocado salsa, garnished with the reserved chilli slices and some coriander sprigs.

Variation: Mexican Soup with Tomato and Chilli Salsa

Prepare the soup as in the main recipe and serve it with the following salsa. Put 150 g (5 oz) chopped tomatoes into a bowl. Add ½ small chopped onion, 1 small crushed garlic clove, 1 deseeded and finely chopped fresh chilli, a pinch of sugar and a few sprigs of coriander. Season with salt and pepper and mix together well.

Devilled oysters

Oysters have long had the reputation of being blessed with aphrodisiac qualities. Try them and see ...

120

12 small oysters, shucked (opened)
1 tablespoon red wine vinegar
1 teaspoon Worcestershire sauce
a few drops of Tabasco sauce
25 g (1 oz) butter
1 shallot, finely chopped
1 garlic clove, crushed
50 g (2 oz) piece pancetta or smoked
   bacon, finely chopped
50 g (2 oz) fresh white breadcrumbs
2 tablespoons freshly grated Parmesan
   cheese
1 tablespoon chopped parsley
a little olive oil
salt and pepper

1 Carefully strain the juices from the oysters into a bowl and stir in the vinegar, Worcestershire sauce and Tabasco sauce. Cut through the muscle that attaches the oyster to the other half of the shell.

2 Melt the butter in a small pan and fry the shallot and garlic for 5 minutes. Add the pancetta or bacon and stir-fry for a further 3–4 minutes until browned.

3 Add the breadcrumbs and pour in the oyster juice mixture; boil until the liquid has nearly all evaporated. Remove from the heat and stir in the Parmesan and parsley and season to taste with salt and pepper. Leave to cool.

4 Arrange the oysters in a baking dish and top each one with the breadcrumb mixture. Drizzle over a little olive oil and cook under a preheated grill for 3–4 minutes until bubbling and golden. Serve the oysters immediately.

Serves 2

Nigiri sushi

Light and flavourful with sensuous seafood, Japanese sushi both looks and tastes divine: perfect for a light supper on a special evening when you have other things on your mind.

123

250 g (8 oz) Japanese short-grain rice, rinsed

275 ml (9 fl oz) cold water

15 g (½ oz) sugar

2 teaspoons salt

2 tablespoons Japanese rice vinegar

1 tablespoon wasabi paste

250 g (8 oz) assorted seafood: thin slices of raw tuna, salmon or
    mackerel; scored and cooked squid; cooked, peeled tiger prawns

To serve:

pickled ginger

wasabi paste

soy sauce

1 Put the rice in a heavy-based saucepan with the cold water. Cover the pan, bring to the boil and simmer for 20 minutes or until the rice is tender and the water absorbed. Remove from the heat, cover the pan with a tea towel and leave to stand for 10 minutes.

2 Put the sugar, salt and vinegar into a small saucepan and heat gently until the sugar has dissolved.

3 Turn the rice out of the pan into a large bowl, sprinkle with the sweetened vinegar and toss gently with two forks to mix the vinegar dressing into the rice and to separate the grains as they cool.

4 Once cool, shape walnut-sized balls of rice into ovals with wet hands. Spread a little wasabi over the top of the shaped rice and arrange a piece of fish or seafood on the top of each one. Arrange on a platter and serve with pickled ginger, extra wasabi and soy sauce.

Spinach pancakes and asparagus gratin

1   First make the pancake batter. Sift the flour and salt into a bowl and make a well in the centre. Gradually beat in the egg. Squeeze the excess liquid from the spinach then chop it very finely. Beat it into the mixture with the milk and beat to form a smooth batter. Cover and leave to rest for 20 minutes.

2   Trim the asparagus spears and blanch in a large pan of lightly salted, boiling water for 2 minutes. Drain, refresh under cold water and pat dry on kitchen paper.

3   Meanwhile, make the pancakes. Heat a little oil in an 18 cm (7 inch) frying pan until it starts to smoke. Pour a ladleful of batter into the pan and swirl to cover the base in a thin even layer. Cook for 2–3 minutes until set, then flip with a palette knife and cook the second side for 1–2 minutes. Remove from the pan and keep warm while cooking the remaining 3 pancakes. Brush the pan with a little oil before adding each ladleful of batter.

4   Place 3 asparagus spears on each pancake and roll up. Place the pancakes seam side down in an oiled baking dish.

5   To make the topping, melt the butter in a small pan, then stir in the flour and cook over a gentle heat for 2 minutes. Gradually whisk in the milk, then slowly bring to the boil, stirring frequently, until the sauce thickens. Stir in the mustard powder and mace and simmer very gently for 5 minutes. Season to taste with salt and pepper.

6   Pour the white sauce over the pancakes and scatter the cheese on top. Place under a preheated medium-hot grill and cook for 8–10 minutes until bubbling and golden. Serve immediately.

Asparagus is reputed to have aphrodisiac qualities, so give it a whirl. If it doesn't work, it still tastes delicious in these pancakes.

125

12 thick asparagus spears
vegetable oil, for greasing

Pancakes:
50 g (2 oz) plain flour
pinch of salt
½ egg, lightly beaten
50 g (2 oz) frozen spinach, defrosted
150 ml (¼ pint) milk
vegetable oil, for frying

Topping:
25 g (1 oz) butter
25 g (1 oz) flour
300 ml (½ pint) milk
½ teaspoon mustard powder
½ teaspoon ground mace
50 g (2 oz) Cheddar cheese, grated
salt and pepper

Crispy wrapped prawns

Cuddle up on the sofa together and share a plate of these scrumptious prawns – who knows what mood you'll be in afterwards?

75 g (3 oz) minced pork

4 raw prawns, shelled and minced

½ teaspoon sugar

¼ onion, finely chopped

1 garlic clove, finely chopped

2 teaspoons light soy sauce

12 raw tiger prawns

12 spring roll wrappers

beaten egg white, for sticking

about 750 ml (1¼ pints) oil

basil or coriander sprigs, to garnish

sweet and sour sauce or chilli sauce, to serve

1 In a bowl, mix the minced pork, minced raw prawns, sugar, onion, garlic and soy sauce then set aside.

2 Shell the other 12 prawns, leaving the tails intact, and carefully cut open the flesh, making sure you do not cut right through the prawns.

3 Put 1 teaspoon or more of the minced mixture on to each open prawn. Take a spring roll wrapper and fold it almost in half, so that one corner is about three-quarters of the way towards the opposite corner. Place a prawn on the double thickness of wrapper, leaving the tail free, and roll it up, tucking the ends in and sticking the wrapper down with a little egg white. Continue until all the prawns are wrapped.

4 Heat the oil in a wok and deep-fry the prawn rolls until golden – this should take about 5 minutes. Remove from the wok and drain on kitchen paper.

5 Garnish the prawns with basil or coriander sprigs and serve with a dipping sauce.

Griddled lobster tails with oregano butter

An expensive dish for a celebration, this should make your loved one feel as though you've made a special effort.

50 g (2 oz) butter, softened
large handful of oregano, chopped
2 lobster tails, halved lengthways
salt and pepper

To serve:
1 lemon, cut into wedges
crisp salad
new potatoes

1 Put the butter and oregano in a bowl, mix together and season to taste with salt and pepper. Place the butter in a rough sausage shape on some greaseproof paper, roll up and twist the ends tightly then place in the freezer to chill and harden for 10 minutes.

2 Heat a griddle pan or nonstick frying pan until hot. Place the lobster tails in the pan and cook for 5 minutes on each side. The shell will turn bright pink and the flesh white.

3 Place the lemon wedges in the pan for 3 minutes to warm the juice.

4 Serve the lobsters with the lemon wedges and accompanied by a salad and new potatoes. Remove the oregano butter from the freezer. Slice and arrange on top of the cooked lobsters to serve.

A Thai-inspired recipe. Creamy coconut milk vies for attention with fiery chillies and lime. It tastes as delicious as it looks.

Coconut grilled chicken

2 boneless chicken breasts

Marinade:

400 ml (14 fl oz) can coconut milk
4 garlic cloves
4 small green or red chillies
2.5 cm (1 inch) piece of fresh root ginger, peeled and sliced
grated rind and juice of 1 lime
2 tablespoons palm sugar or light muscovado sugar
3 tablespoons light soy sauce
1 tablespoon fish sauce
25 g (1 oz) coriander leaf, stalk and root

To garnish:
1 red chilli, deseeded and finely diced
spring onion slivers

1 To make the marinade, blend together all the ingredients.

2 Make 3 oblique cuts on each side of the chicken breasts, put them in a dish and pour the marinade over. Cover and leave in the refrigerator for 2 hours.

3 Arrange the chicken pieces in a grill pan, making sure they are fairly thickly spread with the marinade. Grill under a preheated hot grill for about 15 minutes, turning occasionally. The skin side will take a little longer to cook than the other side.

4 Meanwhile, heat the remaining marinade in a small saucepan until piping hot, adding a little water if it is too thick, to make a pouring sauce.

5 When the chicken is cooked, cut it into slices and arrange them on a serving dish. Serve garnished with spring onion slivers and diced chilli, with the sauce in a separate bowl.

Duckling flavoured with peppercorns and double cream makes this a richly sumptuous dish.

Duckling with peppercorns

1 kg (2 lb) oven-ready duckling

15 g (½ oz) butter

2 shallots, finely chopped

75 ml (3 fl oz) dry white wine

2 tablespoons brandy

1 tablespoon whole green peppercorns or
   ½ tablespoon black peppercorns, coarsely
   crushed

200 ml (7 fl oz) double cream

salt and pepper

chervil, to garnish

green beans, to serve (optional)

Oven temperature: 200°C (400°F), Gas Mark 6

1   Prick the skin of the duckling with a fork and season liberally with salt and pepper. Place in a roasting tin and cook in a preheated oven, 200°C (400°F), Gas Mark 6, for about 1¼ hours until tender.

2   Meanwhile, melt the butter in a saucepan, add the chopped shallots and cook until transparent. Stir in the white wine and brandy, bring to the boil and boil for 5 minutes.

3   Cut the duckling into pieces, arrange on a warmed serving dish and keep hot. Add the peppercorns and cream to the sauce and season with salt to taste. Cook over a low heat for 3–5 minutes until thickened.

4   Spoon the sauce over the duckling and serve immediately, garnished with chervil. Green beans may be served as an accompaniment, if liked.

Grilled beef with spicy sauce

Steak in a spicy sauce is an old favourite, which will put your loved one in the mood for romance, no questions asked. Not for the faint-hearted, though.

300 g (10 oz) sirloin steak

Spicy sauce:

½ tomato, finely chopped

¼ red onion, finely chopped

1 tablespoon dried ground chilli

6 tablespoons fish sauce

2 tablespoons lime juice or tamarind water

2 teaspoons palm sugar or light muscovado sugar

1 tablespoon chicken stock or water

To garnish:

basil leaves

coriander leaves

flat leaf parsley

chillies

1　Put the steak under a preheated hot grill and cook, turning it once, according to your taste. Cook for 6 minutes for a medium-rare steak.

2　While the steak is cooking, mix together all the sauce ingredients in a bowl.

3　When the steak is ready, slice it up and arrange on a warmed serving dish and garnish with the basil, coriander leaves, parsley and chillies. Serve the sauce separately.

Passion cake is so-called for very good reasons: grated carrots and walnuts combine to make a moist, mouth-watering cake with a creamy, smooth soft cheese icing.

Passion cake

150 g (5 oz) butter

200 g (7 oz) light soft brown sugar

175 g (6 oz) grated carrots

½ teaspoon salt

1 teaspoon ground mixed spice

2 eggs

200 g (7 oz) self-raising flour

2 teaspoons baking powder

125 g (4 oz) shelled walnuts, finely chopped

25 g (1 oz) shelled walnut halves, to finish

Icing:

250 g (8 oz) full-fat soft cheese

2–3 tablespoons lemon juice

50 g (2 oz) icing sugar, sifted

Cooking temperature: 180°C (350°F), Gas Mark 4

1 Grease a 20 cm (8 inch) round cake tin and line with greased greaseproof paper.

2 Melt the butter and pour into a mixing bowl. Beat in the sugar, carrots, salt, mixed spice and eggs.

3 Sift the flour and baking powder together and add the chopped walnuts. Lightly fold into the carrot mixture until evenly mixed.

4 Pour the mixture into the prepared tin. Bake in a preheated oven, 180°C (350°F), Gas Mark 4, for 1 hour until firm to the touch and golden brown.

5 Leave the cake to cool in the tin for 5 minutes, then turn out and cool completely on a wire rack.

6 To make the icing, beat the cheese until smooth. Gradually beat in the lemon juice to taste, then beat in the icing sugar until well mixed.

7 Split the cake into two layers and sandwich the layers with one-third of the icing. Spread the remaining icing over the top and sides of the cake and mark wavy lines in it with a fork. Sprinkle the top of the cake with the walnut halves.

Chocolate meringue stacks

Chocolate is a time-honoured arouser of passions, and served in a sauce with these meringue stacks, you should get your way every time …

2 egg whites

125 g (4 oz) caster sugar

1 tablespoon cocoa powder, sifted

grated chocolate and chocolate shapes,
   to decorate

Bitter chocolate sauce:

175 g (6 oz) plain chocolate, broken into pieces

150 ml (¼ pint) water

1 teaspoon instant coffee powder

50 g (2 oz) sugar

Filling:

150 ml (5 fl oz) double cream

2 tablespoons brandy

1 teaspoon clear honey

Oven temperature: 120°C (250°F), Gas Mark ½

1 Whisk the egg whites until stiff, then whisk in the sugar, 1 tablespoon at a time, until the mixture holds its shape. Carefully fold in the cocoa.

2 Line 2 baking sheets with baking parchment and carefully draw eight 7.5 cm (3 inch) and eight 5 cm (2 inch) circles on the paper.

3 Put the meringue into a piping bag fitted with a 1 cm (½ inch) plain nozzle and pipe the meringue into the circles to cover them completely. Bake in a preheated oven, 120°C (250°F), Gas Mark ½, for 2 hours. Transfer to a wire rack to cool.

4 Meanwhile, make the bitter chocolate sauce. Place all the ingredients in a small pan and heat gently until the sugar has dissolved. Bring to the boil and simmer gently for 10 minutes.

5 To make the filling, whip together the cream, brandy and honey until the mixture thickens and holds its shape, then spoon three-quarters of it on to the large meringue circles. Cover with the small circles.

6 Serve the meringue stacks on individual plates and decorate with the remaining cream. Spoon some of the bitter chocolate sauce around each one and sprinkle with a little grated chocolate and decorate with a chocolate shape.

Champagne makes everyone feel romantic at the best of times, and blue Champagne is even more special.

Preparation time 2 minutes **Serves** 1

140

Blue champagne

4 dashes blue Curaçao
125 ml (4 fl oz) chilled Champagne or sparkling white wine

1 Swirl the Curaçao around the sides of a Champagne flute or wine glass. Pour in the Champagne and serve immediately.

Red kiss

Preparation time 3 minutes Serves 1

High romance: vermouth, gin and cherry brandy are stirred together and decorated with cocktail cherries and spirals of lemon rind. A kiss, anyone?

3 ice cubes, cracked

1 measure dry vermouth

½ measure gin

½ measure cherry brandy

To decorate:

1 cocktail cherry

spiral of lemon rind

1 Put the ice cubes into a mixing glass, add the vermouth, gin and cherry brandy and stir well. Strain into a chilled cocktail glass and decorate with the cherry and lemon spiral.

index

143